FALL IN OIL PRICES

The Global Implications

By

Buchi Nwadiuto

DEDICATION

This book is dedicated to countries whose economy is highly dependent on oil.

PREFACE

The oil industry, with its history of booms and busts, is in its deepest downturn since the 1990s, if not earlier.

Earnings are down for companies that made record profits in recent years, leading them to decommission more than two-thirds of their rigs and sharply cut investment in exploration and production. Scores of companies have gone bankrupt and an estimated 250,000 oil workers have lost their jobs.

The cause is the plunging price of a barrel of oil, which has fallen more than 70 percent since June 2014.

Prices recovered a few times last year, but a barrel of oil has already sunk this year to its lowest level since 2004. Executives think it will be years before oil returns to $90 or $100 a barrel, a price that was pretty much the norm over the last decade. In early 2015, IMF management established an interdepartmental working group to develop an integrated institutional view on developments in oil and other key energy markets, and their implications for policy advice to member countries. This paper brings together contributions of the working group to date as well as related work by staff that has appeared in recent IMF publications. IMF staff will continue to provide research and policy analysis on this topic

Table of Contents

CHAPTER ONE

INTRODUCTION--5

CHAPTER TWO

HISTORY OF RISE AND FALL OF OIL-------------8

CHAPTER THREE

RUSSIA, VENEZUELA AND SAUDI ARABIA-----10

CHAPTER FOUR

DISSECTING THE FALL IN OIL PRICES-----------14

CHAPTER FIVE

IMPLICATIONS FOR RETAIL FUEL PRICES AND
PUBLIC FINANCES--19

CHAPTER SIX

MACROECONOMIC IMPLICATIONS OF LOWER
OIL PRICES---24

CHAPTER SEVEN

IMPLICATIONS OF LOWER OIL PRICES FOR THE
FINANCIAL SECTOR------------------------------------31

CHAPTER EIGHT

POLICY RESPONSE TO LOW OIL PRICES---------37

CHAPTER ONE
INTRODUCTION

The unexpected fall in world market prices for oil in the second half of 2014 is comparable to two other recent episodes: in 1986 and 2008–09. The price drop has lowered the cost of living and increased real incomes for consumers in countries where the price declines have been passed on to users. Similarly, firms using oil in production have benefited from lower input prices in these countries. The implied decline in firms 'marginal costs should translate into lower producer prices for their goods and services. These real income gains should result in higher spending and, other factors unchanged, a boost to global growth. This "demand channel" plays an important role in the transmission of the fall in oil prices, and much depends on how large the real income gains are. But the flipside to windfall gains is the income losses of oil producers. The full global economic impact depends on a number of factors, including the nature and magnitude of the oil price decline and the size of the price decline experienced by oil users, among others. Starting with the nature of the oil price decline, two aspects are critical.

☐ Underlying drivers of the price decline. Lower oil prices can be a cause ("shock") driving global economic activity or a response to other shocks driving global growth. In the former, the decline is driven by factors not related to current global economic conditions, say changes in oil supply due to technology. In the latter, the lower prices would be a symptom of other unexpected changes to global economic activity, including, for example, a demand shock in a major economy with significant spillovers to many other economies. Identifying the reasons for the oil price decline is thus critically important for assessing its likely global economic impact. Section II on oil and other energy prices suggests that a large share of the recent oil price decline—likely more than one-half—was due to supply factors. Another aspect is the Persistence of the oil price decline. The effects will also depend on whether the lower oil prices will be temporary or permanent. If temporary, the real income gains (which accrue mainly to the private sector in advanced oil-importing countries) will mostly be saved or, in the case of real income losses in oil exporters (which accrue mainly to the public sector),borrowing will increase. If permanent, spending patterns will need to adjust. The persistence of the oil price decline will depend importantly on the underlying drivers, as well as the adjustment in oil markets to the unexpected decline in prices. Technological progress shifting oil supply, for example, usually results in permanent price changes. But there might be feedback effects, including through investment in oil exploration and development, partly offsetting the longer-term oil price impact. Section II notes that a substantial part of the oil price decline is expected by market participants to persist into the medium term, but there is considerable uncertainty.

Another critical factor for the impact is the extent of price pass-through. Put simply, the issue is how much of the decline in world crude prices translates into a drop in petroleum prices at the retail level. The often small initial pass-through observed in practice partly reflects the usual short-term price rigidities or exchange rate fluctuations, or both. But in many emerging market and developing economies, administrative controls on energy prices, often in the context of fuel price subsidies, provide for more sustained limited pass-through. With limited pass-through, some of the real income gains will accrue to the government or energy companies, rather than households and other end users. The distribution will depend on the specifics of the subsidy and pricing regimes. The macroeconomic impact will then depend not only on the spending behavior of households and firms, but also on the fiscal policy response to such oil-related windfall gains (for instance, the government could either save the windfall, cut distortionary taxes, or invest in highly productive infrastructure) or factors affecting the spending behavior of energy companies. In the extreme, if there were no price pass-through to end users and if the government or energy companies saved all the windfall gains, there would be no transmission to demand channels, although even then there could be benefits through lower government borrowing costs, improved financial balance sheet positions, and confidence effects.

CHAPTER TWO
SHORT HISTORY OF RISE AND FALL OF OIL

This wasn't always the case. Between 2010 and 2014, as you can see above, oil demand was soaring around the world, as countries recovered from the financial crisis but global production was struggling to keep up. Many older oil fields were stagnating. Conflicts in places like Libya and Iraq were restricting supply. Countries had to draw down their stockpiles, and prices soared to around $100 per barrel.

Those high prices, however, spurred drillers in the United States to use innovative hydraulic fracturing and horizontal drilling techniques to unlock vast quantities of oil from shale formations in places like North Dakota and Texas. It's hard to overstate the impact of the boom: US crude oil production has nearly doubled since 2010.

Eventually, supply caught up with demand — and then surpassed it. That's when the crash came.

By mid-2014, global demand was starting to slow down. Europe was still reeling from the Eurozone mess. China's economy was starting to stumble. But the United States continued to produce more and more oil. Iraq and Libya were also starting to bring more production back online. So prices began sliding, down to $70 per barrel.

At that point, many people expected Saudi Arabia and other oil producers in OPEC to cut back on their own production to prop up prices, as they have in the past.

(Conventional wisdom had held that Saudi Arabia needed $100 per barrel oil to balance its budget.)

Surprisingly, that didn't happen. Saudi Arabia decided to increase production in order to maintain its market share, hoping that the subsequent fall in oil prices would crush US frackers, who require higher prices to stay profitable.

CHAPTER THREE
RUSSIA, VENEZUELA AND SAUDI ARABIA

Russia is one of the world's largest oil producers, and its dramatic interest rate hike to 17% in support of its troubled Rouble underscores how heavily its economy depends on energy revenues, with oil and gas accounting for 70% of export incomes.

Russia loses about $2bn in revenues for every dollar fall in the oil price, and the World Bank has warned that Russia's economy would shrink by at least 0.7% in 2015 if oil prices do not recover.

Despite this, Russia has confirmed it will not cut production to shore up oil prices. "If we cut, the importer countries will increase their production and this will mean a loss of our niche market," said Energy Minister Alexander Novak.

Falling oil prices, coupled with western sanctions over Russia's support for separatists in eastern Ukraine have hit the country hard. The government has cut its growth forecast for 2015, predicting that the economy will sink into recession.

Former finance minister, Alexei Kudrin, said the currency's fall was not just a reaction to lower oil prices and western sanctions, "but also [a show of] distrust to the economic policies of the government".

Given the pressures facing Moscow now, some economists expect further measures to shore up the currency.

"We think capital controls as a policy measure cannot be off the table now," said Luis Costa, a senior analyst at Citi.

While President Putin is not using the word "crisis", Prime Minister Dmitry Medvedev has been more forthright on Russia's economic problems.

"Frankly, we, strictly speaking, have not fully recovered from the crisis of 2008," he said in a recent interview.

Because of the twin impact of falling oil prices and sanctions, he said the government had had to cut spending. "We had to abandon a number of programs and make certain sacrifices."

Russia's interest rate rise may also bring its own problems, as high rates can choke economic growth by making it harder for businesses to borrow and spend.

Venezuela

Venezuela is one of the world's largest oil exporters, but thanks to economic mismanagement it was already finding it difficult to pay its way even before the oil price started falling.

Inflation is running at about 60% and the economy is teetering on the brink of recession. The need for spending cuts is clear, but the government faces difficult choices.

The country already has some of the world's cheapest petrol prices - fuel subsidies cost Caracas about $12.5bn a year - but President Maduro has ruled out subsidy cuts and higher petrol prices.

"I've considered as head of state, that the moment has not arrived," he said. "There's no rush, we're not going to throw more gasoline on the fire that already exists with speculation and induced inflation."

The government's caution is understandable. A petrol price rise in 1989 saw widespread riots that left hundreds dead.

Saudi Arabia

Saudi Arabia, the world's largest oil exporter and OPEC's most influential member, could support global oil prices by cutting back its own production, but there is little sign it wants to do this.

There could be two reasons - to try to instill some discipline among fellow OPEC oil producers, and perhaps to put the US's burgeoning shale oil and gas industry under pressure.

Although Saudi Arabia needs oil prices to be around $85 in the longer term, it has deep pockets with a reserve fund of some $700bn - so can withstand lower prices for some time.

"In terms of production and pricing of oil by Middle East producers, they are beginning to recognize the challenge of US production," says Robin Mills, Manaar Energy's head of consulting.

If a period of lower prices were to force some higher cost producers to shut down, then Riyadh might hope to pick up market share in the longer run.

However, there is also recent history behind Riyadh's unwillingness to cut production. In the 1980s the country did cut production significantly in a bid to boost prices, but it had little effect and it also badly affected the Saudi economy.

CHAPTER FOUR
DISSECTING THE FALL IN OIL PRICES

Oil prices fell by about 50 percent between June 2014 and January 2015. The drop consisted of several phases. The initial gradual slide was from $110 a barrel of Brent oil in June 2014 to $80 a barrel before the OPEC meeting in late November. Subsequently, the Brent oil price fell sharply to below $50 a barrel by early January 2015, before recovering partly to about $65 a barrel in May 2015. By contrast, medium-term Brent futures did not materially drop below the established$90–$100 a barrel range until after the OPEC meeting, when they adjusted rapidly to about $70–$75 a barrel, and have stayed in this new range since the first half of December, notwithstanding the sizable rally in spot prices since the start of the year

Both supply and demand factors contributed to the sharp drop in oil prices, but supply factors have played a somewhat more prominent role.

☐ Analysis of revisions to International Energy Agency's (IEA) demand and supply projections points to significant roles for both. Higher supply projections resulted from positive non-OPEC developments (especially U.S. shale oil) and better-than-expected OPEC output in Iraq, Libya, and Saudi Arabia. Weaker-than-expected demand stemmed mainly from Europe and Asia.

☐ Following the decision by OPEC in late November not to curtail oil production, which took markets by surprise, prices fell quickly by about 20 percent as markets fundamentally changed expectations about future OPEC supply. Medium-term oil futures also adjusted sharply.

Econometric techniques, such as univariate regressions with a measure of global economic activity or vector error auto regressions, place a larger weight on supply factors than on demand factors in explaining the oil price fall, as discussed in the April 2015 edition of the WEO. The limitation of these econometric approaches is that they do not allow for the role of changes in expectations and strategic behavior, including by OPEC.

Recent oil price swings may have been exacerbated by changes in financial investors' sentiment, but it is hard to find strong evidence to support the view that speculation or financialization drove the price movements. Non-commercial trading of oil futures and options—that is, trading by players other than those producing or consuming the oil—has increased sharply over the past decade, and shifts in aggregate noncommercial positions may have exacerbated oil price swings.5 Indeed, the sharp drop in spot oil prices at end-2014/early 2015, which was mostly reversed in subsequent weeks, took place at a time when equity prices of energy firms—which in principle reflect expectations of longer-term oil prices that have an important bearing on oil companies' profitability—were broadly flat.6 That said, the oil price drop of the past year has broadly reflected oil market fundamentals.

While the swings in investment positions of noncommercial players in futures markets have attracted attention, the following examples underscore the difficulty in identifying the role of financial investors in driving commodity prices:

☐ In late 2014, oil prices and energy companies' stocks diverged to an unusual degree. At the same time, however, the net long position of speculative players increased even as oil prices continued to fall. This suggests that, at least during this episode, investors' financial flows were not driving the direction of oil price swings.

☐ In April 2015, by contrast, oil prices rebounded despite an oversupplied market. It is difficult to assess whether this was due to purely financial factors or news pointing to a future tightening of oil market balances.

Oil Price Outlook

The degree of the drop in oil prices was not predicted by the futures markets, and caught most forecasters by surprise. Consensus Forecasts showed nobody predicting a steep price fall in August 2014 and only one institution adjusting its forecast to about $50 a barrel in October, shortly before the OPEC meeting. Institutions using models also missed the price fall. This again illustrates the well-known difficulty of forecasting oil prices, given low price elasticities of supply and demand and hard-to-project strategic behavior of key market players.

Over the next several years, futures markets predict a gradual increase in Brent oil prices to about $75 a barrel, although with the typical wide degree of uncertainty. The price uncertainty results from OPEC supply (reflecting both strategic behavior and geopolitical factors), non-OPEC supply (in particular, adjustment of unconventional production to the price drop), and demand (uncertainty about global growth prospects and policies). While there is some evidence that oil investment is adjusting to the new price environment (for example, announced reduction in investment plans by major oil companies and the number of U.S drilling rigs), with capacity already in place from previous large investments, oil production will likely take time to adjust to the new, low price environment, as was the case in the 1980s when non-OPEC production continued to grow in the early years of the price decline. That said, the shorter-term investment horizon of nontraditional production may result in quicker adjustment.

IMF staff are developing a supply-demand model for predicting oil prices. The model weighs the gradual depletion of conventional oil stock against new discoveries and demand trends. It predicts rising oil prices over the medium term, so that sufficient investment takes place to expand supply capacity to meet growing demand. At the same time, illustrative scenarios show enormous uncertainty around the fundamental forces at play. These include energy efficiency, substitution from oil to other energy sources, and climate change policies.

Spillover to Prices of Other Energy Commodities

Natural gas prices have also moved downward, with a differentiated impact across regional markets. Despite the wide differentials in natural gas price levels across continents due to region specific factors, the evidence suggests gas prices tend to follow oil prices with a lag, implying the prospect of further softening in the months ahead. In North America, expanding shale gas production had significantly pushed down prices relative to other regions, well before the decline in oil prices. Limited infrastructure has hindered exports, although several liquefied natural gas (LNG) terminals are slated to open in the near future. Existing production has remained economical partly due to the byproduct nature of natural gas in oil production. In Europe, contracts are typically long term, with fixed volume and adjustable prices indexed to oil prices with a lag. Natural gas prices have decreased in Europe also, partly due to imports of U.S. coal displaced from electricity generation by cheap shale gas. In Asia, natural gas supply relies primarily on Middle Eastern LNG, with a growing share of Australian suppliers. Asian prices are also indexed to crude oil. The benchmark price for Asian LNG has remained elevated since the Fukushima disaster, but spot prices have already decreased dramatically in recent months. Coal prices are formally not linked to oil prices but have followed oil, given substitution opportunities and a common cycle. Coal prices have been declining since early 2011, partly because of the slowdown in emerging markets and displacement by cheap natural gas in the United States.

CHAPTER FIVE
IMPLICATIONS FOR RETAIL FUEL PRICES AND PUBLIC FINANCES

A. Pass-Through into Retail Fuel Prices Lower global crude oil prices have not fully passed through to domestic retail prices. The extent to which domestic prices respond depends on price setting (market-based versus regulated), tax structure, and policy responses. Analysis of retail price data suggests that the median pass through to gasoline and diesel prices was about 50 percent in the second half of 2014.

The pass-through has, so far, been similar to the second half of 2008 (40 percent), when international prices also fell sharply. The pass-through is likely to increase further as countries continue to adjust, for instance, due to formula-based pricing. Over longer periods, the pass-through tends to be higher (for example, the pass through was 80 percent between end- 2008 and mid-2014).

There are wide differences across regions. The Middle East and sub-Saharan Africa have had the lowest pass-through. This reflects a larger incidence of countries with regulated prices. Europe, where prices are largely liberalized, has the highest median pass-through. In general, advanced economies tend to have higher pass-through than emerging markets and developing countries.

There are also large differences within regions, partly reflecting discretionary policy responses to fiscal pressures or fuel pricing reforms. For example, the pass-through was significantly negative (domestic prices rose) in Ghana, Angola, and Cameroon, and to a lesser degree in Brazil and Mexico. In others, the pass-through was positive and higher than the median (for example Zambia and Guinea-Bissau);

B. Impact on Public Finances

Net fuel taxes rose in 2014, reflecting the partial adjustment in domestic prices.12 The rise has been across all regions with the exception of Europe (which has the highest level of net taxes and the highest pass through).In the Middle East and Central Asia, the median net fuel taxes on major fuel products (diesel and gasoline) turned slightly positive by end-2014—still, net taxes remained the lowest. In several countries with regulated prices, subsidies turned to positive net taxes thanks to the sizable fall in international prices

The fiscal savings can be potentially large if the pass-through remains low. The estimates of fiscal savings reflect changes in both explicit and implicit subsidies (and taxes) and not just budgetary subsidies (that is, the estimated savings reflect the cost/saving from the higher/lower gap between international and domestic prices). In the case of oil exporters, the "fiscal savings" may not impact the budget (quasi-fiscal activities) or, if they do, will mostly be reflected as a lower fall in oil-related revenue than what would be implied from the drop in oil prices.13 Middle East countries, where fuel prices tend to be low, are the ones that could potentially generate the largest fiscal savings. Still, countries across different regions (for example, Iran, Venezuela, and Croatia) have high costs associated with low fuel prices (more than 2 percent of GDP) However, the savings could be partly reversed if there is no policy action. Despite some progress in reforming energy prices, most recent fiscal gains resulted from the partial pass through to domestic prices. Based on past episodes, countries—especially oil importers—will tend to adjust domestic prices further over time, leading to lower fiscal savings. In countries with regulated prices, the savings could vanish (at least partially) when oil prices rebound.

Most countries in sub-Saharan Africa (AFR) regulate fuel prices with discretionary adjustments, resulting in a low pass-through to the fall in oil prices. Slightly more than half of African countries regulate fuel prices in a discretionary way, while 40 percent rely on automatic adjustment formulas. Retail prices fell in most countries in the second half of 2014, but at a slower pace than the drop in international prices. In some countries (Angola, Cameroon, Ghana, and Madagascar), domestic prices rose in the context of fuel pricing reforms. As in other regions, the pass-through among net oil exporters was smaller (close to zero)

Price adjustment mechanisms among countries in the Western Hemisphere (WHD) vary widely, with about one-third allowing domestic fuel prices to be fully market determined. The remainder is split between countries with discretionary price adjustment and those where prices are adjusted through a formula. In addition to countries with market determined prices, about one-quarter of countries in the regulated-prices category (for example, Chile, Costa Rica, and Guatemala) are also expected to allow full pass-through. Overall, it is expected that about two-thirds of countries in the region will allow a full pass-through by December.

In some countries, the drop in international prices led to elimination of net subsidies. For example, Mexico has maintained a system of variable excises. When international fuel prices are high, these excises turn into a subsidy, and when prices are low, they turn into a tax. Under this system, there have been no fuel subsidies in Mexico since December 2014, and the increase in fiscal revenues from these excises offsets an important fraction of the decline in export-related fiscal revenues. The Mexican authorities plan to fully liberalize domestic fuel prices in 2018.

Some countries are adopting reforms to reduce subsidies:

□ Losses at Jordan's electricity company (NEPCO) are falling at a faster pace thanks to lower oil prices. Until 2010, the electricity company had a balanced budget when it was receiving gas from Egypt at below-market price. Since then, gas from Egypt has gradually come to a halt, requiring the import of expensive petroleum products. As a result, the company has been running large losses. The authorities have adopted a medium-term energy strategy to return the company to cost recovery. The main elements of the strategy are tariff increases, a diversification of energy sources, and measures to enhance efficiency. Prior to the decline in oil prices, NEPCO's losses were expected to decline from 4½ percent of GDP in 2014 to 3½ percent of GDP in 2015 following a tariff increase and the start of operations of the LNG terminal. However, thanks to the fall in oil prices, additional savings of about 1½ percent of GDP in 2015 are expected.

☐ Egypt is moving forward in reforming energy subsidies. Prior to the reform, in 2013/14, the budgetary cost of untargeted energy subsidies was more than 6 percent of GDP, reflecting their universal provision, as well as high international oil prices. To address the inefficiency and high budgetary costs of generalized subsidies, the authorities decided in July 2014 to drastically raise domestic prices on a range of fuel products. The measure is expected to deliver budget savings of about 2 percent of GDP for 2014/15. The authorities intend to totally eliminate energy subsidies over the next five years, with the exception of those for liquefied pure gas, which are targeted to the poor.

☐ Fuel subsidies in Sudan have significantly declined since 2013. In response to the fiscal pressures, the government of Sudan sharply raised domestic fuel prices in late 2013, reducing subsidies by more than 1 percent of GDP in 2014. The recent decline in international oil prices will further reduce those subsidies, which the authorities plan to eliminate by 2019

CHAPTER SIX

MACROECONOMIC IMPLICATIONS OF LOWER OIL PRICES

According to mainstream macroeconomic models, the fall in oil prices in the second half of 2014 should have resulted in a boost to global economic activity by some ½ percentage point of global GDP in 2015–16, even assuming an incomplete pass-through in most emerging market and developing economies. However, global growth forecasts since the October 2014 WEO have been revised down. This largely reflects negative effects from other shocks, as well as the expectation that much of the windfall income gains from lower oil prices will be saved in many oil-importing economies.

The IMF's G-20 model discusses the likely global macroeconomic effects of the decline in oil prices. The model uses empirical evidence about the effects of oil price changes on household and business behavior, and it takes into account the strong feedback mechanisms between oil prices and global economic developments (and expectations thereof) as the effects of the oil price shock unfold. It also features the interaction between the boost to activity from the oil windfall gains in oil importers and windfall losses in exporters (mainly through trade linkages).

The global economic implications depend on a number of factors. Two are of particular relevance and explored in the scenario analysis:

☐ The drivers and magnitudes of the oil price decline. There is strong evidence of an important supply component in the large oil price decline since June 2014. Specifically, the scenarios assume that the price decline was driven by a persistent, but not fully permanent, oil supply shock. The shock was calibrated such that it generates an oil price path that matches the difference between the oil price baseline assumptions in the April 2015 WEO and the October 2014 WEO (40 percent lower in 2015, moderating gradually to about 20 percent by 2020).

☐ Incomplete price pass-through. As illustrated in Section III, many governments control the domestic prices of petroleum products through a variety of instruments. The oil windfall gains or losses do not fully accrue to the private sector, but to fiscal or quasi-fiscal authorities, including state-owned energy companies.

The decline in world oil prices is passed on fully to households and firms in all countries. While very stylized, it provides a useful point of reference. The second scenario broadly replicates the current pricing regimes discussed in the previous section. In advanced economies, the pass-through is complete. In most emerging market and developing economies and in oil producers, it is incomplete. The simulation results confirm that global output effects depend on the degree of price pass-through. If the decline in global oil prices since August 2014 were to fully pass through to domestic end-user prices, global GDP—excluding those countries in which oil supply is increasing—would rise by roughly 1 percent in the first two years . If the decline in oil prices were to fail to fully pass through and the resulting increase in fiscal revenue were to be saved, the increase in global GDP would be reduced by almost half.16 The simulations illustrate how in countries with managed retail prices, the boost to growth can be much more modest . The growth effect would be larger if the government used the windfall to cut distortionary taxes or make efficient investments. More limited pass-through would also moderate the impact of the decline in oil prices on global inflation, albeit by a relatively small margin. Revisions to WEO forecasts since October 2014 have not resulted in predictions of higher global growth during 2015–16. Instead, global growth projections have been modestly revised down. Those for oil exporters have been lowered substantially, as was to be expected, while those for emerging market and developing oil importers have also been lowered or unchanged, rather than increased. On the other hand, the downward revisions to price levels have been substantial, as have the revisions to fiscal balances of oil exporters. The revisions to fiscal balances of oil importers were small on average, given high pass-through of lower oil prices to retail prices in advanced economies, and adverse shocks affecting growth in emerging markets and developing countries. The decline in oil prices, which began in June 2014, has also not resulted in higher global growth in that year, relative to what was expected before the decline, including relative to forecasts in the April 2014.

What explains this apparent disconnect between simulations and revisions to projections?

Staff analysis points to the following factors:

☐ Other shocks. Many major economies have experienced other shocks, ranging from the implications of the Ukraine conflict for Russia to stronger-than-expected effects of fiscal consolidation in Japan. Also, the deceleration in growth in China is expected to continue, and conflicts in the Middle East have intensified. Such decline in activity due to other shocks has contributed to the oil price decline. Model simulations confirm that in scenarios where the increased oil supply explains much—but not all—of the oil price decline in 2014 because of other adverse demand shocks in some economies, these adverse demand factors can broadly offset the positive impact of the oil supply shock. This reflects the fact that the positive effects of even large oil price changes on activity in oil importers are relatively small because the share of oil in total expenditure and costs is small, even in relatively oil-intensive economies. In addition, activity in some commodity exporters many be held back by the simultaneous drop in non-oil commodity prices.

☐ Initial conditions. Interactions between initial conditions can lead to situations where lower oil prices will have a smaller impact on spending by households and firms. In particular, in view of still unresolved balance sheet strains after the global financial crisis in some advanced economies, some of the real income (windfall) gains in these economies will be used to retire debt, rather than be spent.

☐ Policy responses. In a number of oil-importing economies, IMF staff assume that governments or state-owned energy companies will save the oil windfall gains not only initially, as assumed in the simulations, but more permanently. Put differently, the oil windfall gains offer authorities an opportunity to help improve their fiscal positions without hurting domestic demand. In fact, without the windfall gains, the positions would have deteriorated, given other shocks. The backdrop to this strategy is the deterioration in fiscal positions in many emerging market and developing economies before the decline in oil prices. As macroeconomic vulnerabilities have become more costly with increased capital flow reversal risks in these economies, authorities have sought to reduce such vulnerabilities. Similar considerations apply to state-owned energy companies, which had seen their financial positions deteriorate as they bore the costs of increased energy subsidies in recent years. The implied increase in national savings explains the projected improvements in current account balances in these economies. IMF staff will prepare an assessment of the actual macroeconomic impact of lower oil prices on several large economies, with expected publication in the October 2015 WEO.

The large, abrupt oil price decline since June 2014 has been among the three largest declines over the past three decades. The other declines of similar magnitude were recorded in 1986, when OPEC members partly reversed previous production cuts, and in 2008–09 during the early stages of the global financial crisis.

The reasons for the price drop have differed across these cases. The big-picture view is that in 1986, price declines were mostly supply-driven while in 2008–09, they were almost entirely demand-driven. Evidence to date suggests that supply factors have been important for

the 2014 price decline The differences in underlying drivers can be seen clearly in the differences in output behavior in advanced economies across episodes. Growth was broadly stable in the first year for the price declines in 1986 and 2014, while output contracted sharply in 2008–09. It is noteworthy, however, that there appears to be no sign of activity picking up in the first year of each price decline, not only since June 2014, but also in 1986. Monthly industrial production growth remained broadly flat, as did quarterly GDP growth. The price pass-through, as measured by headline CPI inflation, was strong and immediate in each case. In fact, the inflation response in the current episode appears somewhat weaker. Another area where strong responses are apparent is current account balances, where the external positions of exporters worsen and those of importers improve.

A counterfactual forecasting exercise for economies in the Asia and Pacific region illustrates the important role of initial conditions and precautionary policy responses to oil windfall gains for the small growth impact in economies in the region. For this exercise, IMF staff revised their October 2014 macroeconomic forecasts under the assumption that the oil price decline was the only change in assumptions. All other assumptions remained the same as they were for the October projections. The increase in both private and public net saving ratios is striking. On the other hand, growth is broadly unchanged, because a sizable part of the windfall to net oil (and commodity) importers is expected to be saved, increasing current account surpluses.

CHAPTER SEVEN
IMPLICATIONS OF LOWER OIL PRICES FOR THE FINANCIAL SECTOR

While the recent decline in oil prices will benefit the global economy as a whole, the speed and magnitude of the price drop could trigger financial strains in several areas. This section discusses three potential sources of financial vulnerabilities that could yet play outgoing forward:

☐ A self-reinforcing cycle of rising credit risk and deteriorating refinancing conditions for countries and companies with substantial exposures to the oil sector;

☐ A decline in oil-related financial surplus recycling in global funding markets; and

☐ Strains in the ability of the financial market infrastructure to accommodate a prolonged period of heightened energy price volatility.

The financial sector implications appear manageable overall, but there are downside risks. Countries and companies dependent on oil revenues have already been significantly re-priced, especially those with existing vulnerabilities, but the impact may not yet have been fully felt. A redistribution of wealth among investors with varying savings and portfolio preferences could also have market repercussions. Regarding concerns about market infrastructure, there does not appear to be evidence of dislocations in the oil markets so far.

A. Amplification of Credit Risk

Risk premiums on countries and companies dependent on oil revenues have widened since the summer of 2014, as reflected in bond spreads, equity prices, and currency movements. However, there are risks related to refinancing of energy-exporting sovereigns, corporate credit issuance, and severing of bank funding lines to energy companies in response to breaches of lending covenants.

□ Country refinancing risk. Fiscal breakeven prices vary widely across oil-producing countries in emerging markets, from US$57 per barrel for Kuwait, up to US$206 per barrel for Libya. Unless spending cuts are enacted, new sources of revenues are established, or fiscal buffers are tapped, the loss in oil revenues will result in a need for new sources of financing. U.S.-dollar-based bond spreads for emerging market oil-exporting countries have widened materially in many—but not all—cases since summer 2014, suggesting refinancing conditions have become more problematic. Local currency depreciation may also put upward pressure on inflation where domestic inflation expectations are not well anchored. This could further raise the risk premium on sovereign debt, although depreciation would also improve the fiscal position of oil exporters.

□ Corporate refinancing in the energy sector. The scaling back of energy sector exposure by banks and corporate bond investors could amplify strains associated with falling revenues and higher funding costs. Historically, corporate defaults in the energy sector have tended to pick up in response to falling oil prices with a lag of about 12 months, likely reflecting a typical one-year hedging horizon used by producers (Fitch, 2015). Because the downdraft in oil prices began to accelerate only in September 2014—at which point Brent and WTI prices were still above $100 per barrel— aftershocks for the corporate sector may yet remain.

A prolonged period of low oil prices will put at risk the debt servicing capacity of exploration and production firms with a high cost base. The outstanding worldwide notional value of bank loans and corporate debt extended to the energy sector amounts to about US$3 trillion, US$247 billion of which is attributable to the U.S. high-yield bond market alone. Global issuance in 2014 was substantially higher than during the previous cycle peak in 2007

Additionally, the leveraged (that is, high-yield) share of syndicated oil and gas loan issuance has steadily increased, from 17 percent in 2006 to 45 percent in 2014. While the majority of global systemically important banks appear to have only about 2–4 percent of their total loan book exposure devoted to the energy sector, some emerging market and U.S. regional banks reportedly have much higher exposures (albeit, firm estimates are difficult to establish).

A reduction in investors' exposure to highly leveraged companies may have knock-on effects on investment and, eventually, on oil extraction. For instance, Russian companies have increased capital expenditure in line with their leverage over the past 10 years. With financing drying up, companies are expected to cut their capital expenditure by 10–15 percent in 2015, possibly leading to lower oil production in future years.

In some countries (for example, in the Caucasus and Central Asia), a decline in remittance flows from oil-producing countries has contributed to exchange rate pressures, bringing to the fore financial stability risks in their banking systems. In the Middle East and North Africa region, oil price declines led to broad-based declines in stock prices of oil-exporting countries, while government deposits in commercial banks have begun to be drawn down.

B. Oil Surplus and Global Liquidity

Foreign exchange reserves accumulated by net oil-exporting countries have increased US$1.1 trillion, or almost fivefold, over the past decade. Accounting for about 15 percent of the cumulative rise in world foreign exchange reserves since 2004, these funds have constituted an important source of funding for the global banking sector and capital markets. Deposits from oil-exporting countries in banks reporting to the Bank for International Settlements (BIS) have doubled to US$972 billion since 2004, and this group of countries (private and public sector) now holds more than US$2 trillion in U.S. assets spread across equities (US$1.3 trillion), Treasuries (US$580 billion), credit (US$230 billion), and debt instruments issued by U.S. government-sponsored enterprises (US$21 billion). Following the US$88 billion contraction in oil exporter reserves in

2014, further significant declines in 2015 are to be expected, given the oil price outlook. In principle, the decline in investable oil surpluses is part of a global rebalancing and ought to be counterbalanced—at least to an extent—by wealth gains on the part of oil importers. But such redistribution between agents with potentially varying savings and portfolio preferences may have market repercussions, particularly if the pace of adjustment creates dislocations. The rebalancing could result in modest upward pressures on global long-term real interest rates.

C. Strains on Financial Infrastructure

Oil and other commodity markets have attracted much greater focus from the institutional investment community over the past decade. For example, noncommercial (that is, speculative) investors held about 45 percent of WTI futures contracts in 2014, about three times the share during the 1990s. Exchange-traded products based on oil and other commodities have also risen in size over the same period, making the asset class accessible to retail investors. At the same time, banks have retreated from their market-making and structuring roles in energy markets, with a shift in trading activity to centrally cleared contracts—as desired by regulators and the U.S. Dodd-Frank legislation—and physical commodity trading houses. With such significant changes in market structure, concerns arise as to whether a heavy wave of selling coupled with a reduced ability of banks to accommodate increased trading volumes result in disorderly market conditions. To be sure, there has already been substantial selling—for example, net investment positions of noncommercial investors in the oil futures market were cut by nearly half during the second half of 2014. In addition, data from prospectuses available in early 2015 suggest U.S. high-yield bond funds have already adopted an underweight position in energy, vis-à-vis their benchmarks. Assets under management in commodity funds, combined with commodity-linked exchange traded products, have also nearly halved from their peak levels of 2010. On balance, however, there does not appear to be evidence that the unwinding of positions in the oil markets has led to dislocations in market functioning. Measures of intraday volatility are within historical norms, and while measures of forward-looking implied volatility (which reflect insurance value) have increased to levels recorded in 2011–12, they remain well shy of those in 2008, when markets were highly stressed. While commodity exchanges have a long history of managing counterparty risk and periods of heightened volatility (that is, through changes in margining requirements and circuit breakers), financial intermediaries would be wise to stay on alert for threats to market functioning.

CHAPTER EIGHT
POLICY RESPONSE TO LOW OIL PRICES

Policy responses to lower oil prices, which are still being formulated in many countries, will depend on a complex set of factors. These include, for example, the size and direction of the terms-of-trade shock, the exchange rate regime, fiscal and external buffers, balance sheet mismatches, exchange rate valuation, the output gap, and inflation. To organize ideas, we propose a flexible policy framework to determine the appropriate mix of adjustment of fiscal, monetary, and exchange rate policies. The framework—presented for clarity in a Venn diagram—frames choice through lenses of fiscal vulnerabilities, external vulnerabilities, and the cyclical position, and is sufficiently flexible to allow for other country-specific circumstances such as the net direction of oil trade and exchange rate regime.

A. Oil Exporters

Since the oil price drop is expected to have a large permanent component, policies of oil exporters should focus on fiscal adjustment, supported by stronger medium-term fiscal frameworks. Oil receipts fell dramatically even for those exporters that increased oil production; should oil prices turn out to be higher than the baseline projection, many exporters would still have their fiscal breakeven prices well above the usual range of oil price forecasts. How quickly the adjustment should proceed, and how far it needs to go, will depend on the size of buffers (fiscal vulnerability) and the scale of oil reserves. In addition, exporters with external vulnerabilities should consider depreciation and/or greater exchange rate flexibility. Strikingly, the largest negative terms of- trade shock has hit countries with fixed exchange rate regimes, putting additional pressure on other policies to deliver the needed adjustment in these countries that tend to be most reliant on oil exports .Monetary policy should strike the right balance between the domestic cycle and the degree of vulnerabilities. Countries exposed to potential financial strains would benefit from strengthening their macroprudential policy frameworks.

☐ Countries outside of the Venn space with comfortable fiscal and external buffers and limited policy risks can adjust to lower oil prices gradually, and use their policy buffers to smooth the transition (for example, Norway).

☐ By contrast, countries at the center of the Venn diagram should start adjusting policies at a brisk pace immediately (for example, Venezuela). Policy choices diverge depending on the exchange rate regime. A flexible exchange rate regime helps partly mitigate the external and fiscal impact of lower dollar oil prices, as long as there are no major foreign exchange balance sheet mismatches resulting, for instance, from a high degree of dollarization. In contrast, a country with a fixed exchange rate regime would need to considerably tighten macro policies (especially fiscal policy), if it wants to maintain its current peg. Moving to a different nominal anchor could—depending on circumstances—reduce the adjustment costs the country faces, for example by facilitating fiscal adjustment if expenditure allocations are held fixed in local currency terms.

☐ Countries with sizable fiscal buffers can consolidate gradually over the medium term and possibly even ease fiscal policy in the short run, to minimize the negative impact of lower oil prices and other adverse shocks on growth. In the presence of existing inflationary pressures or external vulnerabilities, monetary policy will need to remain tight to control inflation expectations and to stem capital outflows.

☐ Some countries highly dependent on energy exports face special circumstances, including several members of the Gulf Cooperation Council. The countries may have accumulated large fiscal and external buffers, but still face the prospect of large medium-term fiscal deficits. Their economies may be characterized by an undiversified structure, reliance on imported labor, strong pass-through of exchange rate changes to import prices, and limited monetary policy infrastructure given long-standing exchange rate pegs. These countries should maintain their currency pegs, but aid both fiscal and external adjustment by formulating adequate medium-term fiscal consolidation plans early on. The pace of adjustment should be gradual, in line with the size of buffers. Low government debt in some of these countries would facilitate issuance of government securities to help finance the fiscal deficits, supporting development of local bond markets.

B. Oil Importers

The key question faced by oil importers, by contrast, is how much of the windfall to save in cases where retail prices do not adjust automatically. In general, lower oil prices will improve household real incomes, corporate profits in the non-oil sector, and fiscal positions where energy subsidies are large. The Venn diagram suggests that the higher the level of vulnerabilities and the more advanced the business cycle, the more of the windfall countries should save to rebuild policy buffers and slow the impact on aggregate demand. Fiscal consolidation policies will generally be easier to implement in the countries where the benefits of lower oil prices accrue mostly to the public sector. Meanwhile, countries should use the period of lower oil prices as an opportunity to strengthen the credibility of their monetary policy frameworks.

Evidence of second-round disinflationary effects could open space for reducing policy rates in some countries, while countries at risk of deflation should loosen monetary policy and save less—or none—of the windfall. There may also be scope in some countries to allocate part of the windfall to investment and social spending.

☐ For countries that are outside of the Venn space, and have a negative output gap, policies should allow domestic demand to rise by the full amount of the windfall (in countries in this situation, but with a high degree of pass-through into retail prices such as the United States, there is no need for policy adjustment). Lower energy prices also provide a window to consider increasing energy taxation while reducing other distortionary taxes or raising priority spending.

☐ For countries with fiscal and external vulnerabilities such as Egypt, priority should be given to putting fiscal and external positions on a more sustainable footing by saving the fiscal windfall from lower energy subsidies, reducing public debt levels, and increasing international reserves as current account positions improve. Some countries can consider raising energy taxes to improve fiscal positions and compensate for negative externalities (adverse effects) from fuel consumption.

☐ For oil importers facing deflationary risks, authorities should not save any of the windfall (again, when the windfall accrues to the private sector, there is no need for active policy measures to adjust public saving) and will need to ensure inflation expectations remain anchored to avoid falling into a debt-deflation spiral, including, if needed, through unconventional monetary policy.

☐ Emerging market economies and low-income countries with policy space should spend part—or all— of their windfalls on longer-term growth-enhancing spending (infrastructure, education, and tax cuts).

C. Medium-Term Policies

Over the medium term, oil exporters would benefit from a number of structural reforms. These reforms are beneficial in their own right, but lower oil prices strengthen the case for commencing implementation early on. The priorities include the following:

□ Fiscal consolidation and frameworks. Fiscal policies should be recalibrated to lower oil prices, with the speed of adjustment determined by the extent of vulnerabilities. The adjustment should favor growth, equity considerations, and developing the non-commodity sector. Most oil exporters also need to either establish, or enhance, their medium-term fiscal frameworks.

□ Diversification. Real and financial sector reforms aimed at strengthening the private sector would help boost non-oil growth.

□ Financial sector policies. Exporters would benefit from strengthening liquidity management, enhancing early-warning systems, addressing concentration risks in the financial system, and deepening the financial sector.

□ More flexible exchange rate regime. Some countries could consider greater flexibility, but others will have to rely almost entirely on fiscal policy adjustment to attain a current account that is consistent with fundamentals and chosen policy settings. The decision (and timing) to move to greater exchange rate flexibility will depend mainly on factors such as the capacity to conduct independent monetary policy, credibility of the peg, financial depth, the degree of economic diversification, and the flexibility of fiscal policy. Where the domestic non-oil sector is small and imports and services provided by foreign workers are very large, exchange rate shifts have a limited role in facilitating the needed adjustment in demand and the external balance.

☐ Reform of energy prices and taxation. Both exporters and importers should take advantage of lower oil prices to remove distortions such as fuel subsidies and should consider increasing energy prices/taxes where appropriate, to create space for accompanying growth enhancing fiscal measures. Targeted mitigation measures and communication strategies will be crucial to secure political buy-in. In a number of low- and middle-income countries, energy sector reforms to broaden access to reliable energy would have important development benefits.

☐ Other considerations. Many countries would benefit from greater fiscal transparency, including by exposing quasi-fiscal activities of the energy-sector state-owned enterprises. Inflation expectations in advanced oil importers need to be closely monitored. Distributional effects of policies (such as the inclusiveness of growth) should also be taken into account.

The low oil prices open a window of opportunity to increase domestic energy prices toward international levels and avoid a large gap reopening in the future. Both oil exporters and oil importers should work toward fully liberalizing domestic prices or adopting automatic pricing formulas to lock in the savings. The use of targeted transfers, financed with fiscal savings from higher fuel prices, would protect the most vulnerable groups. It may also be appropriate to increase energy taxes in many countries. There are both revenue and environmental considerations for this recommendation, including the following:

☐ Strengthening the fiscal position. Resources could be used to reduce fiscal vulnerabilities or to finance key spending priorities (for example, social or investment). In addition, in countries with high unemployment, reductions in labor taxation could be financed through higher taxation of fuel products.

☐ Limiting the negative spillovers (for example, environmental costs and inefficiencies). These are typically larger where fuel products are cheaper, due to higher consumption.

According to the latest IMF estimates, the global costs of low energy prices are sizable.

The "pre-tax subsidies", which arise because the price paid by consumers in some countries is below the opportunity/supply cost, amount to some $330 billion globally. "Post-tax subsidies," which also include the health effects of local pollution, costs of traffic congestion, impact of global warming, and other factors are estimated by Coady and others (2015) at a staggering $5.3 trillion. While these figures are naturally subject to substantial uncertainty, their magnitude highlights the need for urgent policy action in this area. Budget transparency of the costs of low energy prices should also be improved. Budget documents should reflect the true size of implicit and explicit fuel subsidies, allowing a more transparent analysis of the trade-off between budget priorities. Moreover, more transparency of accounts of energy-related state-owned enterprises will help ensure that the portion of the windfall that accrues to them is utilized in a way that is consistent with the overall fiscal strategy.

References

Arezki R., D. Laxton, A. Nurbekyan, and H. Wang. 2015. "An Exploration in the Deep Corners of the Oil Market," IMF Research Bulletin 16(1), pp. 1-4.

Barclays. 2015. "Oil Rally in Perspective," Asset Allocation Research—Investor Intel, May 22.

Benes J., M. Chauvet, O. Kamenik, D. Laxton, S. Mursula, and J. Selody. 2015. "The Future of Oil: Geology versus Technology," International Journal of Forecasting 31(1): 207–21.

Cheng, I.-H. and W. Xiong. 2014. "The Financialization of Commodity Markets," Annual Review of Financial Economics 6: 419–41.

Citibank. 2015. Standpoint: Annual Outlook. Global Market Analysis by Citi EMEA Regional Consumer Bank.

Coady, D., I.W.H. Parry, L. Sears, and N. Shang. 2015. "How Large Are Energy Subsidies?", Working Paper 15/105, International Monetary Fund, Washington, DC.

Fitch. 2015. "Global Crude Fallout," February.

Goldman Sachs. 2015. "Reality of Oil Market Will Trump Perception and Positioning," May 18.

Hunt, B., D. Muir, and M. Sommer. 2015. "The Potential Macroeconomic Impact of the Unconventional

Oil and Gas Boom in the United States," Working Paper 15/92, International Monetary Fund, Washington, DC.

Parry, I. W.H., D. Heine, E. Lis, and S. Li. 2014. Getting Energy Prices Right: From Principle to Practice. International Monetary Fund, Washington, DC.